Episode 1:
To You, 2,000 Years From Now

ATTACK ON TITAN

1

HAJIME ISAYAMA

13

HUH...?!

FWOOOO

845

...I WON'T.

...THAT I WAS CRYING.

DON'T TELL ANYONE...

DON'T BE STUPID! LIKE I CAN TELL MY OLD MAN ABOUT **THIS**?!

WHY DON'T YOU HAVE YOUR DAD EXAMINE YOU?

CRYING FOR NO REASON...

M-MR. HANNES!

!!

WHAT ARE YOU CRYING ABOUT, EREN?

...THAT HASN'T HAPPENED IN A HUNDRED YEARS!

BUT I TELL YA...

IF THE BASTARDS BREAK THROUGH THE WALL, WE'LL BE ON TOP OF THE SITUATION.

HAHAHA... THE DOCTOR'S SON HAS SPIRIT!

HEY, EREN! DON'T SUDDENLY RAISE YOUR VOICE LIKE THAT...

I'M NOT GONNA SECOND-GUESS DR. YEAGER, THIS TOWN'S BENE-FACTOR.

BUT Y'KNOW...

WELL... YOU MAY BE RIGHT.

MY FATHER SAYS SO!!

B-BUT IT'S DANGEROUS TO FEEL AT EASE LIKE THIS!

WHEN YOU BECOME A SOLDIER, YOU GET YOUR CHANCE TO SEE 'EM, HANGING AROUND OUTSIDE THE WALL WHILE YOU'RE ON WALL DEFENSE DUTY OR WHATEVER...

...AND I JUST CAN'T PICTURE 'EM EVEN PUTTING A DENT IN THIS 50-METER* FORTRESS.

*164 FEET

THAT AIN'T A BAD IDEA EITHER!

W-WHAT THE HELL?! SO STOP CALLING YOURSELVES A "GARRISON" AND MAKE IT THE "WALL CONSTRUCTION CORPS" INSTEAD!

NOPE.

THEN YOU'RE NOT EVEN PREPARED TO FIGHT 'EM IN THE FIRST PLACE, ARE YOU?!

...

ON THE OTHER HAND, WHEN THE GUYS AND I ARE MOCKED AS GOOD-FOR-NOTHING SPONGES, THAT TELLS YOU WE'RE ALL LIVIN' IN A TIME OF PEACE, AM I RIGHT?

YOU HAVE SOLDIERS ON ACTIVE DUTY WHEN THE SITUATION HAS GONE TO HELL...

BUT EREN...

...UHN...

WAA...

...WE WERE ABLE TO GET BACK.

DOOOOO

THAT'S ALL...

WAAAAGH!

WAAAAGH!

...

...BUT...

...MY SON...

UHH... UHH...

...WAS USEFUL TO YOU, WASN'T HE?

...EREN SAID...

YEAH. I HAVE TO SEE A PATIENT TWO TOWNS UP.

HUH? DAD, YOU'RE GOING OUT **NOW?**

M-MIKASA!! I TOLD YOU NOT TO TELL THEM!

EREN!!

...HE WANTS TO JOIN THE SURVEY CORPS.

...

Y-YES, I KNOW!!

DO YOU KNOW HOW MANY PEOPLE HAVE DIED BECAUSE THEY DARED TO VENTURE OUTSIDE THE WALL?!

WHAT ARE YOU THINK-ING?!

...INSIDE THE WALL, IGNORANT OF WHAT'S HAPPENING IN THE WORLD OUTSIDE!!

I HATE THE IDEA OF SPENDING MY WHOLE LIFE...

WHY DO YOU WANT TO GO **OUTSIDE?**

EREN...

AND BESIDES...

...EVERYONE WHO DIED UP TO NOW WILL HAVE DIED IN VAIN!

IF THERE'S NO ONE TO CARRY ON...

WAIT... HONEY!

WELL, I'D BETTER BE GOING. THE BOAT LEAVES SOON.

...I SEE...

"FOOLISH" ...?!

WHAT ?!

...DO ANYTHING AS FOOLISH AS JOINING THE SURVEY CORPS!

I WON'T LET YOU...

EREN... ...

...

...ARE THE REAL FOOLS!

THE WAY I SEE IT... PEOPLE WHO ARE SATISFIED LIVING LIKE CAGED BIRDS...

I WILL!

...SO HELP HIM OUT IF HE GETS IN TROUBLE.

THAT BOY IS FOOLHARDY...

MIKASA...

...AND called me a "HERETIC".

...HE PUNCHED ME...

...SHOULD EVENTUALLY GO TO THE OUTSIDE WORLD...

SO WHEN I SAID THE HUMAN RACE...

PEOPLE ARE AFRAID THAT IF WE GO OUT CARELESSLY, **THEY** COULD GET IN.

WELL... IT'S BECAUSE WE'VE LIVED HERE PEACEFULLY INSIDE THE WALL FOR 100 YEARS NOW.

DAMN IT, WHY DO PEOPLE FROWN ON EVEN THE SLIGHTEST MENTION OF WANTING TO GO "OUTSIDE"?

BUT I WONDER IF THAT'S THE ONLY REASON...

...YOU'RE RIGHT ABOUT THAT.

IN OTHER WORDS, THE KING IS A COWARD!

ROYAL GOVERNMENT POLICY SAYS THAT EVEN HAVING AN INTEREST IN GOING TO THE OUTSIDE WORLD IS TABOO.

WE CAN DO WHAT WE WANT WITH THEM, RIGHT?

THEY'RE **OUR** LIVES!

...NOT!

AB-SOLUTE-LY...

I DON'T REMEMBER AGREEING TO KEEP IT A SECRET.

THAT REMINDS ME, THANKS A LOT FOR RATTING ME OUT TO MOM AND DAD!!

NO WAY.

...

...NATURALLY...

...THEY WEREN'T PLEASED.

OF COURSE

SO... HOW'D THEY TAKE IT?

...BUT COME ON, IT'S DANGEROUS.

LOOK, I KNOW HOW YOU FEEL...

W-WHAT THE HELL?! ARE YOU TELLING ME TO GIVE UP ON IT TOO?!

...THERE'S NO GUARANTEE THAT THEY WON'T BREAK THROUGH IT TODAY, FOR EXAMPLE.

JUST BECAUSE THE WALL HASN'T BEEN BREACHED IN 100 YEARS...

I MEAN, FOR SURE, I THINK THE PEOPLE WHO BELIEVE WE'LL BE SAFE INSIDE THIS WALL FOREVER HAVE A SCREW LOOSE.

ARMIN, WHAT IS IT...?!

H-HEY... WHAT THE HECK ARE YOU LOOKING AT?!

*ABOUT 50 FEET

...AH...

...MADE A HOLE IN THE WALL?!

I-IT...

!! DASH MIKASA!!

MOM'S AT HOME!!

THOSE PIECES OF THE WALL FELL NEAR THE HOUSES!!

FWOOOO

ULP...!!

QUIVER

QUIVER

...

...

WILL BE OVER-RUN BY TITANS!!

THIS TOWN...

IT'S ...TOO LATE...

...GOT INSIDE, DIDN'T THEY?

T-THE TITANS...

HURRY UP!!

I KNOW!

MIKASA, HURRY!!

...I...

NOW!!

!!

EREN!! TAKE MIKASA AND GET OUT OF HERE!!

COME ON!! LET'S GET OUT OF HERE TOGETHER!!

I'D LOVE TO!! SO LET'S HURRY UP AND GET YOU OUT!!

...

I'LL CARRY YOU!!

EVEN IF YOU GET ME OUT, I CAN'T RUN... YOU UNDERSTAND, DON'T YOU?

MY LEGS GOT CRUSHED BY THE RUBBLE.

...THE SURE THING AND JUST RESCUE THE KIDS?

DO I GO WITH...

OR DO I TAKE A CHANCE FIGHTING THE TITAN TO TRY TO SAVE THE THREE OF THEM...?

GLARE

I'M GONNA...

LISTEN TO CARLA...?

OR PAY BACK MY DEBT...?!

SQUEEZE

I...

GUVER

GRAB

?!

CHAK

WHAT ARE YOU DOING?! HEY... MY MOM IS STILL...

M-MR. HANNES ?!

H-HEY!

THANK YOU...

SURVIVE ...!!

EREN!! MIKASA!!

UHN...

...

I'M SORRY...

I'M SORRY...

FwOOOO

THIS AGAIN...

OH...

THROB

ROOOOAAR

WE'RE DE-PART-ING!!

THIS BOAT'S FULL!!

UP TO THE END, ALL I COULD DO WAS ARGUE AND BE STUBBORN!

...TO GO HOME AGAIN.

MOM'S GONE!! I'M NEVER GONNA SEE HER AGAIN...

IS CRYING THE ONLY THING THE WEAK CAN DO?!

IS IT BECAUSE HUMANS ARE WEAK?

WHY IS THIS HAPPENING TO US?

I'M GONNA DESTROY THEM!!

EVERY LAST ONE...

...OF THOSE ANIMALS...

...THAT'S ON THIS EARTH!!

850

GIVEN THE SENSE OF CRISIS AT THE TIME, WE WERE ILL-PREPARED TO COPE WITH THE SUDDEN APPEARANCE OF THE **COLOSSUS TITAN**...

WE HAVE PAID THE PRICE FOR 100 YEARS OF PEACE WITH TRAGEDY.

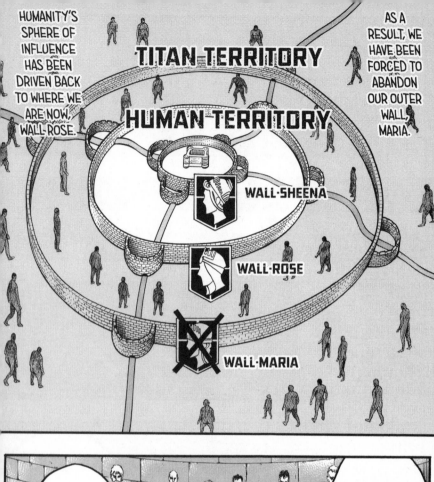

HUMANITY'S SPHERE OF INFLUENCE HAS BEEN DRIVEN BACK TO WHERE WE ARE NOW, WALL-ROSE.

TITAN TERRITORY

HUMAN TERRITORY

AS A RESULT, WE HAVE BEEN FORCED TO ABANDON OUR OUTER WALL, MARIA.

WALL-SHEENA

WALL-ROSE

WALL-MARIA

...TO DESTROY THIS WALL RIGHT THIS MOMENT.

IT WOULDN'T BE A SURPRISE IF THAT COLOSSUS TITAN SHOWED UP...

...AND GIVE YOUR LIVES TO STAND AGAINST THE TITAN MENACE!

WHENEVER THAT TIME DOES COME, YOUR DUTY WILL BE TO RELIEVE THE **PRODUCERS**...

YES, SIR!!!

DEDICATE YOUR HEARTS!!

I WILL NOW ANNOUNCE THE TEN AMONG YOU WHO HAVE OBTAINED THE TOP TRAINING RESULTS. COME FORWARD IF I CALL YOUR NAME.

TODAY, YOU HAVE COMPLETED YOUR MILITARY TRAINING.

Current Publicly Available Information

TOWN

TOWN

TOWN

The reason for having a town jutting out of the main wall

IN THIS WORLD, WALL CONSTRUCTION IS A MATTER OF THE UTMOST IMPORTANCE.

AS ILLUSTRATED BY THE SIMPLE DIAGRAM ON THE LEFT, WITH A TOWN JUST BUILT INSIDE THE WALL, IN THE EVENT THAT THE TITANS BURST THROUGH, THE PEOPLE WOULD HAVE NO MEANS TO COPE WITH THE CRISIS. PUT SIMPLY, WITH SUCH A VAST CIRCUMFERENCE, PEOPLE WOULDN'T KNOW WHERE THE WALL WOULD BE BREACHED. AND NATURALLY, THERE AREN'T ENOUGH HUMANS TO SUPPORT A MILITARY FORCE THAT COULD MONITOR AND GUARD THE ENTIRE RINGED WALL.

IN OTHER WORDS, THE OBJECT IS TO NARROW DOWN THE TARGET. THIS STRATEGY KEEPS THE COST OF GUARDING THE WALL MANAGEABLE AND ALLOWS THE MILITARY TO CONSOLIDATE ITS FORCES. HOWEVER, WITHOUT HUMANS WITHIN THE WALL TO SERVE AS "BAIT" THAT WILL ATTRACT THE TITANS, THIS STRATEGY HAS NO CHANCE OF PAYING OFF. HAVING TROOPS GARRISONED AT THE TOWN GUARANTEES AN ECONOMIC BENEFIT FOR THE AREA, BUT THAT ECONOMIC ADVANTAGE FALLS SHORT WHEN COMPARED TO THE FEAR OF BEING EATEN BY A TITAN. THUS, NOT MANY PEOPLE ARE ENTHUSED ABOUT LIVING IN THESE TOWNS. THEREFORE, THE RULING MONARCHY PRAISES THE RESIDENTS OF THESE FRONT-LINE TOWNS AS "THE BRAVEST OF WARRIORS" IN AN ATTEMPT TO DRUM UP MORE VOLUNTEERS.

A BIT OF HISTORY: SINCE THE STRENGTH OF THE GATES THAT CONNECT THE HUMAN DOMAIN TO THE TITANS' TERRITORY OUTSIDE THE WALLS IS INFERIOR TO THAT OF THE WALL ITSELF, THERE WAS A PROPOSAL BY CONSERVATIVES TO SEAL THE GATES OFF ENTIRELY. HOWEVER, REFORMISTS SUCCESSFULLY ARGUED THAT "ABANDONING THE GATES TO THE OUTSIDE WORLD IS TANTAMOUNT TO ABANDONING THE WILL OF THE HUMAN RACE TO RECLAIM ITS DOMINION" AND THE PLAN WAS HALTED.

AS THE STORY PROGRESSES, MORE LIGHT WILL BE SHED ON HOW THE WALL WAS INITIALLY BUILT AND THE SITUATION AT THE TIME OF ITS CONSTRUCTION.

...YOU HAVE THREE CHOICES.

NOW THAT YOU'VE COMPLETED YOUR TRAINING...

THE **GARRISON,** WHICH REINFORCES THE WALLS, THEREBY PROTECTING ALL OF THE TOWNS...

THE **SURVEY CORPS,** PREPARED TO SACRIFICE THEIR LIVES OUTSIDE THE WALLS BY DEFYING THE TITANS IN THEIR OWN DOMAIN...

AND **THE MILITARY POLICE BRIGADE,** WHICH EXERCISES CONTROL OVER THE KING'S SUBJECTS AND MAINTAINS ORDER...

OF COURSE, OUT OF YOU RAW RECRUITS, THE ONLY ONES WHO **CAN** JOIN THE MILITARY POLICE BRIGADE...

...ARE THE TEN WITH THE HIGHEST SCORES.

HUH?

I'M SURE YOU'RE GONNA JOIN THE MILITARY POLICE BRIGADE, RIGHT?

LUCKY BASTARDS, MAKING THE TOP TEN!

GETTING TO WORK NEAR THE KING... IT'S AN HONOR!!

I'M GOING WITH THE MPs, TOO.

GRAAH!!

THAT GOES WITHOUT SAYING! WHY THE HELL ELSE WOULD I HAVE AIMED TO CRACK THE TOP TEN?!

YOU CAN'T WAIT TO GET INTO THE INTERIOR, RIGHT?

TELL ME HOW YOU REALLY FEEL.

PFFT !!

ARE YOU STILL PLAYING THE GOODY-GOODY, MARCO?

A SAFE, COMFORTABLE LIFE IS WAITING FOR US IN THE INTERIOR, RIGHT?!

WE CAN FINALLY ESCAPE THIS SHITTY, SUFFOCATING FRONT-LINE TOWN!!

I FORGOT YOU WERE A PRIZE PUPIL!

OH, SORRY! MY BAD!

SH-SHAME ON YOU! AT LEAST, I'M NOT...

YOU...

WHA...

SWISH

BUT WHAT WOULD YOU GUYS DO?

OR GIVEN THE CHOICE, WOULD YOU RATHER STAY HERE IN THIS "HUMAN STRONGHOLD", OR WHATEVER THEY LIKE TO CALL IT?!

I MEAN, GETTING THE CHANCE TO LIVE IN THE INTERIOR, IT'S ALMOST UNHEARD OF, RIGHT?!

SO IF IT MEANT NOT HAVING TO COWER IN FRIGHT WHEN YOU HEAR TITAN FOOTSTEPS...

...NONE OF US ASKED TO BE BORN IN THIS BORDER TOWN.

WELL...

SO... HOW ABOUT YOU GUYS?

YOU'D ALL LIKE TO GO TO THE INTERIOR, RIGHT?

GOOD ANSWER...

GREAK

...BUT I DON'T WANT ANYONE TO THINK I'M LIKE **YOU.**

ME TOO...

I'M APPLYING TO THE MILITARY POLICE BRIGADE.

UNTIL FIVE YEARS AGO, **THIS** TOWN WAS PART OF THE INTERIOR, TOO.

...

YOU SAID THE INTERIOR IS COMFORTABLE...?

HEY...

HA HA HA!!

I MEAN, ISN'T THE INTERIOR OF YOUR BRAIN SOFT ENOUGH FOR YOU?

JEAN... YOU DON'T HAVE TO GO TO THE INTERIOR.

DON'T.

...

WAAH...

EREN...

S-SORRY!

UWAAA!

PFFT!

...MORE THAN ANYONE.

WELL, I'M NOT ...I'M LOOKING AT REALITY.

...

...THAT I'M AN IDIOT, EREN?

ARE YOU TRYING TO SAY...

AN ALL-OUT ATTACK WAS LAUNCHED...

FOUR YEARS AGO, TWENTY PERCENT OF THE HUMAN POPULATION WAS SENT OUT TO RECOVER TERRITORY STOLEN BY THE TITANS.

HOW MANY MORE WOULD WE HAVE NEEDED TO RETAKE OUR LAND?

AND MOST OF THEM ENDED UP WALKING STRAIGHT INTO A TITAN'S MOUTH, SWALLOWED WHOLE.

HOWEVER, THE NUMBER OF TITANS WHO DOMINATE THIS PLANET IS A LOT MORE THAN 1/30TH OF THE HUMAN RACE.

FOR EVERY ONE OF THEM THAT WE DEFEATED, AN AVERAGE OF 30 HUMANS DIED.

HUMANITY...

I THINK IT'S CRYSTAL CLEAR.

...DOESN'T STAND A CHANCE AGAINST THE TITANS.

SIGHHH...

SO WHAT?

LOOK... IT'S LIKE A FUNERAL IN HERE, THANKS TO YOU.

...

SO WHAT YOU'RE SAYING IS, "I DON'T THINK WE CAN WIN, SO I'M GIVING UP."

HUH? WERE YOU LISTENING TO ME?

IS IT BETTER TO ESCAPE FROM REALITY, TO THE POINT WHERE YOU'RE THROWING AWAY YOUR HOPE?

TELL ME... WHAT'S SO GOOD ABOUT GIVING UP?

...IT'S A GIVEN THAT WE'D LOSE TO THE TITANS IN MATERIAL TERMS.

IN THE FIRST PLACE...

...

WE LOST THEN, BUT THE INFORMATION WE GAINED WILL SURELY LEAD TO OUR HOPE FOR THE FUTURE.

ONE OF THE CAUSES OF THE DEFEAT FOUR YEARS AGO WAS OUR IGNORANCE ABOUT THE TITANS...

I...

AND YET YOU'RE GOING TO GIVE UP ON DEVELOPING STRATEGIES TO FIGHT THEM? DO YOU WANT TO BE TITAN FOOD THAT BADLY? GIVE ME A BREAK.

I HAVE A DREAM...

IT'S TO EXTERMINATE THE TITANS AND LEAVE THIS CRAMPED WALLED-UP WORLD. MY DREAM IS TO EXPLORE...

...THE OUTSIDE WORLD.

WHAT?!

WHAT THE HELL ARE YOU TALKING ABOUT?! YOU MUST BE THE ONE WITH THE SOFT NOGGIN!

HA!

...

I GOT IT...

OKAY... YOU'RE RIGHT...

LOOK AT THEM! NOT A SINGLE PERSON HERE AGREES WITH YOU!

OF COURSE, THAT'S JUST WHAT I'M GONNA DO, BUT YOU WANNA GO OUTSIDE THE WALL, RIGHT? GO ON AHEAD! THE TITANS YOU MUST LOVE SO MUCH ARE WAITING FOR YOU!

SO SHOVE OFF TO THE INTERIOR... HAVING A DEFEATIST LIKE YOU HERE ON THE FRONT LINE IS BAD FOR MORALE!

HEH...

PAIN IN THE ASS...

WHOK!

THERE THEY GO AGAIN!!

WHOAAA!

...YOU'RE NOT FIT TO GO UP AGAINST THE TITANS!!

ADOOOSH

!!

OF COURSE NOT, IDIOT!!

COME ON, EREN! WHAT'S WRONG?! IF YOU'RE HAVING TROUBLE AGAINST ME, A MERE HUMAN...

?!

THOK

...?!
MIKASA
?!

?!

P-PUT ME DOWN!!

FLAIL FLAIL FLAIL FLAIL

OR, WAIT... WAS HE SECOND TO MIKASA?

LET'S STOP FIGHTING AMONGST OURSELVES!

UM, NO... I THINK WE'VE ALL HAD OUR FILL.

THIS IS THE HIGHLIGHT OF THE FAREWELL PARTY! DON'T STOP ME!!

HEY... FRANZ...!!

JEAN, IF YOU GUYS KEEP MAKING A RACKET, THE INSTRUCTOR'S GONNA COME BY!

TCH.

HAVING MIKASA TO CARRY YOU AROUND LIKE THAT!

YOU'RE LUCKY, EREN!

PUT ME DOWN, MIKASA...!

HEY!

HA HA HA

I BET YOU'RE PLANNING TO DRAG HER INTO THE SURVEY CORPS JUST THE SAME WAY!

YOU ALWAYS ACT IMPULSIVELY WHEN YOU GET ANGRY...

...THAT HURT, DAMMIT!!

THUD

OOF!!

WHICH BRANCH DO **YOU** WANNA ENLIST IN?

ABOUT WHAT HE SAID...

THEY'RE CALLING YOU THE MOST TALENTED PERSON WHO'S EVER BEEN THROUGH TRAINING... I'M SURE YOU'D GET SPECIAL TREATMENT!

YOU WERE AT THE HEAD OF OUR CLASS... APPLY FOR THE MPS!

...

I'M JOINING THE SURVEY CORPS.

ZRUSH

WITHOUT ME AROUND, YOU'LL DIE AN EARLY DEATH.

IF YOU JOIN THE GARRISON...

IF YOU JOIN THE MILITARY POLICE BRIGADE, THEN SO WILL I.

...I'LL DO THE SAME.

I DIED ONCE AND WAS RESTORED TO LIFE. I WON'T FORGET THAT DEBT.

AS LONG AS WE LIVE...

HOW LONG DO YOU INTEND TO KEEP AT THIS?!

I'M NOT ASKING YOU TO STICK WITH ME!

I DON'T WANT TO LOSE ANY MORE FAMILY...

BUT MORE THAN ANYTHING...

OH... HEY, ARMIN...

LET'S GO BACK TO THE DORM.

THE PARTY'S BREAKING UP, YOU TWO...

GFF

...

TOOO

...

WHICH BRANCH ARE YOU GONNA APPLY TO?

ARE YOU SERIOUS?

I MEAN, YOU'RE...

!!

I'M GONNA JOIN THE SURVEY CORPS!

I'M WEAKER THAN THE AVERAGE PERSON.

AND IT WAS A MIRACLE THAT I PASSED THE SIMULATED COMBAT GRADUATION TEST...

YEAH, I KNOW...

MAKING AN INEFFICIENT CHOICE THAT DISREGARDS YOUR STRENGTHS? I WOULDN'T CALL THAT COURA-GEOUS.

...

BUT DIDN'T THE INSTRUCTOR TELL YOU TO BECOME A TECHNICIAN, SINCE YOU'RE ACADEMICALLY AT THE TOP OF THE CLASS?!

...

IF I DIED IT WOULDN'T MATTER!

...

YES, SIR!

ALL RIGHT, YOU'RE DISMISSED FOR TODAY.

BEEN A LONG TIME, HUH...?!

DISCIPLINE IS IMPORTANT, BUT WHEN IT COMES TO YOU GUYS, I JUST CAN'T GET USED TO IT...

UH... AT EASE.

I SEE... IT **HAS** BEEN FIVE YEARS SINCE YOU CAME TO THIS TOWN, HUH?

AH... YOU RUGRATS HAVE GOTTEN BIGGER AGAIN, HAVEN'T YOU?

A DRUNKARD LIKE YOU, NOW A SQUAD LEADER IN THE GARRISON...

I CAN'T GET USED TO IT EITHER...

YOU DIDN'T HAVE A CHOICE.

ENOUGH ABOUT THAT AL-READY.

BEFORE YOU GUYS WERE BORN...

...

...I COULDN'T SAVE YOUR MOTHER.

I'M SORRY...

...

BUT THEN ONE DAY, DR. YEAGER APPEARED WITH THE ANTIBODY FOR IT...

MY WHOLE FAMILY WAS CURED.

...MY FAMILY CAME DOWN WITH THE DISEASE THAT KILLED SO MUCH OF OUR TOWN.

THE ONLY THING TO POSSIBLY GO ON IS YOUR MEMORY, SINCE YOU WERE THE LAST ONE TO SEE HIM...

I STILL DON'T HAVE THE SLIGHTEST CLUE ABOUT WHERE YOUR FATHER, DR. YEAGER, IS.

HOW MANY TIMES DO I HAVE TO HEAR THIS?

I WANTED TO PAY BACK THAT DEBT TO YOUR FAMILY, BUT NOW I'LL NEVER GET THE CHANCE...

THROB

!

!

SLUMP

EREN ?!

DO YOU REMEMBER ANYTHING?

?!

EREN ...!!

BOOM

HOLD OUT YOUR ARM!

YOU WERE CRYING OUT IN YOUR SLEEP. WHAT WERE YOU DREAMING ABOUT?

...ARE YOU OKAY? YOU COLLAPSED RIGHT AFTER THAT, SO WE CARRIED YOU HERE TO THE DORM.

WHAT **WAS** IT ABOUT? ...HUH...? I FORGOT ALREADY.

...WE'RE GETTING MORE PEOPLE.

THEY MAY CALL IT A FRONT-LINE TOWN, BUT...

Y'KNOW...

NOT TO MENTION WE'VE MADE THE WALL A LOT STRONGER THESE PAST FIVE YEARS.

MAYBE THAT COLOSSUS TITAN HAS GIVEN UP ON US...

WELL, NOTHING **HAS** HAPPENED FOR FIVE YEARS NOW.

PEOPLE CANNOT LIVE IN FEAR FOREVER.

...

YOU'RE GETTING AHEAD OF YOUR-SELF, EREN!

TO EVEN THINK WE'D MAKE A GOOD COUPLE...

WH-WHO SAID WE WERE MARRIED...?!

GRAB

MARRIAGE HAS TURNED YOU SOFT!

WHAT'S THAT FOOLISH CRAP?!

HUH?!

YOUR SPEECH LAST NIGHT HAD AN EFFECT ON HIM.

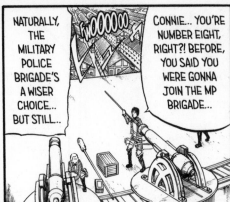

FMOOOOOO

NATURALLY, THE MILITARY POLICE BRIGADE'S A WISER CHOICE... BUT STILL...

CONNIE... YOU'RE NUMBER EIGHT, RIGHT?! BEFORE, YOU SAID YOU WERE GONNA JOIN THE MP BRIGADE...

S-SHUT THE HELL UP!! I DECIDED FOR MYSELF!

THAT DOESN'T EXPLAIN WHY YOU'D JOIN THE SURVEY CORPS...

I JUST DON'T WANNA BE IN THE SAME BRANCH AS THAT BASTARD!

W-WRONG!! I... IT WAS...THAT'S RIGHT! IT WAS JEAN!

BESIDES, YOU'RE NOT THE ONLY ONE...

PARDON ME, BUT...

FOO

DON'T BE SO EMBARRASSED! SOMETIMES EVEN WHEN YOU KNOW WHAT YOU **SHOULD** DO, YOU STILL HESITATE TO FOLLOW THROUGH.

I BORROWED A LITTLE MEAT FROM THE SENIOR OFFICERS' PRIVATE STOCK.

...

SCARY DUMB.

YOU KNOW, YOU REALLY ARE DUMB.

BUZZ BUZZ

SASHA... YOU WANNA GET THROWN INTO SOLITARY...?

...

CLINK

DON'T WORRY.

THAT'S RIGHT! EVER SINCE OUR TERRITORY SHRANK, MEAT HAS BECOME INCREDIBLY PRECIOUS!

PUT IT BACK!

LET'S SPLIT IT UP LATER. SLICE IT, SLAP IT BETWEEN SOME BREAD... HEEHEEHEE...

HUH?

I SEE YOUR POINT.

...WE'LL BE ABLE TO KEEP MORE COWS AND SHEEP AGAIN.

ONCE WE RECAPTURE OUR TERRITORY...

ONCE WE EAT IT, ALL THAT'S LEFT IS PREPARING OURSELVES FOR THE WORST!!

IT'LL BE LIKE A CELEBRATION IN ANTICIPATION OF REGAINING WALL MARIA.

...

...

THOMAS...

...

?

I'LL EAT THAT MEAT, TOO!!

...THE HUMAN RACE IS TAKING BACK ITS DIGNITY.

FINALLY, AFTER LOSING A THIRD OF OUR TERRITORY AND 20% OF THE POPULATION...

WE CAN WIN...

HUMANITY'S COUNTERATTACK...

...BEGINS NOW!

SAMUEL!
DON'T
MOVE!

UNH...

UNHHH...

FWOOOO

OOOO

GRRRRM

...LAST ONE!!

EVERY...

SASHA!!

DAMMIT... THE TITANS REALLY ARE GONNA...

AGAIN... THE TITANS ARE GONNA COME IN AGAIN...

BOOOM

IT BROKE THROUGH THE WALL...

PRE-PARE FOR COMBAT!!

?!

FIXED ARTILLERY SQUAD 4!

TAKE CARE OF SAMUEL!!

Weight-Shifting Equipment for Vertical Maneuvers

COMPLEX WEIGHT-SHIFTING TECHNOLOGY THAT EMPLOYS FULL BODY-ENCOMPASSING FIXED BELTS IS REQUIRED TO MAKE VERTICAL MANEUVERS POSSIBLE.

NORMALLY STORED IN THE SIDE HOLDER

OPERATING DEVICE

ATTACHED TO THE WAIST

ATTACHED TO THE THIGH

SCABBARD

VERTICAL MANEUVER DEVICE

THE LIGHTWEIGHT EQUIPMENT IS DESIGNED FOR HIGH-SPEED, THREE-DIMENSIONAL MOBILITY.

THE PERSON SHIFTS THEIR ENTIRE WEIGHT TO EITHER SIDE OF THEIR HIPS. THE MAJORITY OF THAT WEIGHT IS APPLIED TO THE BOTTOM OF THEIR OPPOSING FOOT. THOUGH THE MANEUVERS GIVE THE APPEARANCE OF EFFORTLESS FLIGHT THROUGH THE AIR, IT'S A SYSTEM THAT ONLY WORKS THROUGH STRENUOUS USE OF MUSCLES THROUGHOUT THE USER'S BODY.

Episode 4:
First Battle

Current Publicly Available Information

A Basic Overview of the Vertical Maneuvering Devices

THE OPERATING DEVICE IS RUN BY A BLACK BOX (TECHNICAL SPECS, MAINTENANCE AND IMPROVEMENT OF THESE SPECS ARE SECRET).

MAIN TAP CONNECTED TO THE CYLINDER

(THE VERTICAL MANEUVERING DEVICE)

STEEL WIRE IS STORED IN THE OPERATIVE SECTION

CONNECTED TO THE BELT

CONNECTED TO THE OPERATING DEVICE

TWO AXES SPIN INDEPENDENTLY

STEEL WIRE TO PIERCE TITANS, ETC.

GAS IS BLOWN DIRECTLY AT THE FAN TO MAKE IT SPIN.

THE PART THAT BLOWS GAS TOWARDS THE FAN AND THE EMISSION SYSTEM ARE BLACK BOXES (TECHNICAL SPECS, MAINTENANCE AND IMPROVEMENT OF THESE SPECS ARE SECRET).

EXHAUST

THE EMISSION SYSTEM IS SHAPED LIKE A SHUTTLECOCK SO IT DOESN'T INTERFERE WITH THE GAS COMING IN THROUGH THE INTAKE PORT.

(PARTS OF THE FAN)

GAS PRESSURE IS ADJUSTED TO MANAGE THE OUTPUT.

THE GAS IS COMPRESSED INTO THE CYLINDER, THEN INJECTED INTO THE TUBE.

THANKS TO MY SCIENTIST FRIEND WHO HELPED ME COME UP WITH THIS!

BASTARD...

AND THAT'S NOT ALL!

IT WAS NO COINCIDENCE THAT HE WENT FOR THE GATE EITHER!!

HE AIMED FOR THE FIXED ARTILLERY...!!

...INTELLIGENT.

THEN HE IS...

THUD

THUMP

NHH!!

...

EREN! DID YOU KILL IT?!

THE COLOSSUS TITAN DISAPPEARED!!

HE SUDDENLY APPEARED AND SUDDENLY VANISHED...!!

NO... IT'S JUST LIKE FIVE YEARS AGO...

HEY... IS THIS ANY TIME TO CHAT?!

WHAT ARE YOU APOLOGIZING FOR? WE COULDN'T EVEN MOVE...

...I'M SORRY. I LET HIM GET AWAY...

!!

WHAT ARE YOU TRAINEES DOING?!

IF IT ISN'T PLUGGED UP FAST, WE'LL GET ANOTHER TITAN INCURSION!!

PART OF THE WALL'S ALREADY DESTROYED!

PLEASE EVACUATE CALMLY!

LEAVE ALL MATERIAL POSSESSIONS BEHIND!

THEREFORE, WE IN THE GARRISON ARE CURRENTLY ALONE IN REPAIRING THE WALL AND PREPARING FOR AN INCURSION.

REGRETTABLY, THE SURVEY CORPS, WHICH HAS THE MOST ACTUAL COMBAT EXPERIENCE, IS OUTSIDE THE WALL ON AN EXPLORATORY EXPEDITION.

THIS IS YOUR FIRST OPERATION, BUT WE EXPECT YOU TO CONTRIBUTE!

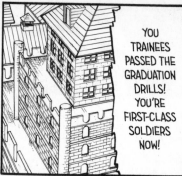

YOU TRAINEES PASSED THE GRADUATION DRILLS! YOU'RE FIRST-CLASS SOLDIERS NOW!

...

! ...

FRANZ...

DON'T WORRY, HANNAH... I SWEAR I'LL PROTECT YOU.

I-I'M FINE! I'M SURE THINGS WILL SETTLE DOWN SOON!

...

ARMIN, ARE YOU ALL RIGHT?!

EREN!

THEY PUT THAT ROCK THERE TO PLUG A HOLE, BUT WE CAN'T EVEN MOVE IT!

S-STILL... THIS ISN'T GOOD! WE'VE STILL GOT AN EIGHT-METER HIGH HOLE IN THE WALL AND NO WAY TO FIX IT QUICKLY!

...IF THE TITANS FELT LIKE IT...

...THEY COULD EXTERMINATE THE HUMAN RACE AT ANY TIME!!

AND THE MOMENT WE REALIZE WE CAN'T FILL IN THE HOLE, THIS TOWN WILL BE ABANDONED... AFTER THAT, IT'S ONLY A MATTER OF TIME BEFORE THEY GET THROUGH WALL ROSE... TO BEGIN WITH...

S-SORRY. I'M FINE...

...

CALM DOWN!!

AH!!

ARMIN!

YOUR DUTIES ARE SUPPORT, COMMUNICATIONS, TITAN-KILLING AND ANYTHING ELSE THAT'S NEEDED.

JUST LIKE IN YOUR TRAINING, EACH SQUAD WILL TAKE A DIFFERENT STREET. YOU'RE UNDER GARRISON COMMAND.

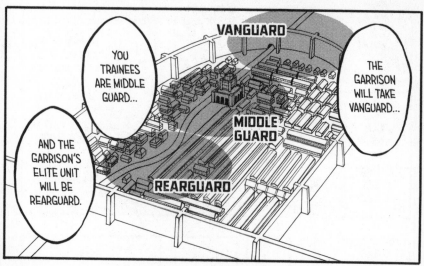

VANGUARD

MIDDLE GUARD

REARGUARD

YOU TRAINEES ARE MIDDLE GUARD...

THE GARRISON WILL TAKE VANGUARD...

AND THE GARRISON'S ELITE UNIT WILL BE REARGUARD.

...UNTIL EVERY LAST MAN, WOMAN AND CHILD HAS SAFELY EVACUATED.

TIME FOR US FREELOADERS TO PAY OUR TAB. WE'VE GOTTA DEFEND WALL ROSE TO THE DEATH...

BE PREPARED TO SACRIFICE YOUR LIVES, PEOPLE.

OH, AND AS YOU'RE AWARE, DESERTING IN THE FACE OF THE ENEMY IS CONSIDERED A CAPITAL OFFENSE.

YES, SIR!!

FWAP

DIS-MISSED!!

I'M SUPPOSED TO GO TO THE INTERIOR TOMORROW!!

WHY DID IT HAVE TO BE TODAY...?!

SLUMP

URRGGH!!

ARE YOU ALL RIGHT?!

BLEEGH

URK...

UP!

?!

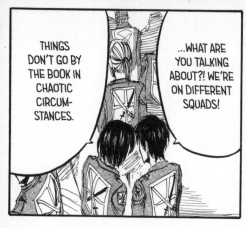

THINGS DON'T GO BY THE BOOK IN CHAOTIC CIRCUMSTANCES.

...WHAT ARE YOU TALKING ABOUT?! WE'RE ON DIFFERENT SQUADS!

HUH?!

IF THE BATTLE GETS HAIRY, FIND ME.

TRAINEE MIKASA!!

WHAT IS THIS "PROTECTION" STUFF ABOUT...?!

...

I'LL PROTECT YOU!

...

GET ON OVER THERE!!

YOU'VE BEEN SPECIALLY ASSIGNED TO REARGUARD!

HEY!

B-BUT ...!

THE EVAC'S GOING SLOWLY RIGHT NOW, SO WE NEED THE BEST OF THE BEST GUARDING THE PUBLIC!

I'M NOT ASKING YOU YOUR OPINION!

?!

...WITH MY SKILL, I'D ONLY BE IN THE WAY!

HUMANITY IS ON THE BRINK OF EXTINCTION AND YOU'RE TRYING TO DICTATE YOUR OWN RULES?!

THAT'S ENOUGH, MIKASA!

?!

I WASN'T THINKING WITH A CLEAR HEAD...

SORRY...

...

BUT... I DO HAVE A FAVOR TO ASK... JUST ONE... PLEASE...

DON'T DIE...

I CAN'T DIE HERE.

I WON'T DIE...

FwOOOo

I STILL DON'T KNOW ANYTHING ABOUT THE WORLD OUTSIDE OUR WALL...

EVEN IN OUR REMAINING HISTORY BOOKS, NOTHING IS WRITTEN ABOUT THE ORIGIN OF THE TITANS. WE KNOW NEXT TO NOTHING ABOUT THEM.

THEREFORE, THERE IS NO PRECEDENT FOR MUTUAL UNDERSTANDING BETWEEN OUR RACES.

WE HAVEN'T BEEN ABLE TO CONFIRM WHETHER THE TITANS POSSESS HUMANLIKE INTELLIGENCE.

WHAT WE'VE LEARNED ABOUT THE TITANS, SUCH AS THEIR MODE OF LIFE, WE OWE TO THE LATEST REPORTS BY THE SURVEY CORPS.

THEIR BODIES HAVE EXTREMELY HIGH TEMPERATURES AND, STRANGELY, THEY SHOW ABSOLUTELY NO INTEREST IN LIFE FORMS OTHER THAN HUMANS.

THE STRUCTURE OF THE TITAN BODY IS FUNDAMENTALLY DIFFERENT FROM OTHER LIVING BEINGS... THEY HAVE NO SEXUAL ORGANS AND THE METHOD BY WHICH THEY REPRODUCE IS UNKNOWN. MOST OF THEM TEND TO HAVE A MALE PHYSIQUE.

...BUT WHEN WE CONSIDER THAT THEY EXISTED IN AN ENVIRONMENT DEVOID OF PEOPLE FOR OVER 100 YEARS... WE MAY MAKE THE CONJECTURE THAT TITANS DON'T ACTUALLY **NEED** TO EAT.

THE TITANS' SOLE BEHAVIORAL PRINCIPLE IS EATING HUMAN BEINGS...

...BUT RATHER PURELY KILLING.

OR IN OTHER WORDS, THEIR PURPOSE ISN'T PREDATORY...

...IS THE TITANS' ASTOUNDING ABILITY TO SURVIVE.

...THE MAIN REASON THE HUMAN RACE HAS BEEN DRIVEN INTO A CORNER...

ALSO...

THERE ARE INDIVIDUAL DIFFERENCES, BUT IN MOST CASES, HEADS THAT ARE BLOWN OFF REGENERATE IN ONE TO TWO MINUTES.

HOWEVER, THAT ALONE WASN'T ENOUGH TO COPE WITH THEM.

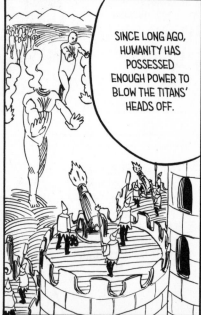

SINCE LONG AGO, HUMANITY HAS POSSESSED ENOUGH POWER TO BLOW THE TITANS' HEADS OFF.

...ARE THE TITANS INVULNERABLE?!

TEACHER! SO THEN...

LIKE IT'S NOT BAD ENOUGH THAT THEY'RE HUGE...

...I DON'T BELIEVE IT...

AIM FOR RIGHT HERE!!

THERE'S ONE WAY TO FELL A TITAN.

NO, THEY'RE NOT INVULNERABLE...

IF A TITAN SUSTAINS MAJOR DAMAGE HERE, IT DOESN'T REGENERATE, BUT DIES.

THIS AREA BELOW THE OCCIPITAL REGION, AT THE NAPE OF THE NECK.

AT PRESENT, THE MOST EFFICACIOUS MEANS OF REPELLING THE ENEMY IS THROUGH COMBAT SKILLS THAT MAKE THE BEST USE OF MOBILITY.

FOR THAT VERY PURPOSE, YOU MUST ALL MASTER THIS **VERTICAL MANEUVERING EQUIPMENT.**

STEEL WIRE DISCHARGED FROM INSIDE A CYLINDER IS REELED IN THROUGH PRESSURIZED GAS.

THE FIRING MECHANISM AT BOTH SIDES OF THE WAIST LAUNCHES AN ANCHOR.

EACH HAND USES THE GRIP OF THIS DEVICE TO OPERATE THE SYSTEM.

IN ORDER TO CUT THROUGH A CHUNK OF TOUGH MEAT, THE BLADE IS MADE TO BE FLEXIBLE.

THIS REPLACEABLE BLADE IS YOUR WEAPON.

IF THE ATTACK HITS THE TITAN'S VITAL SPOT, IT DIES INSTANTLY, BEFORE ITS REGENERATIVE SYSTEM CAN KICK IN.

YOU USE THESE TWO BLADES TO SLICE THROUGH THE AREA.

...WE CAN BE USEFUL.

FINALLY...

FINALLY...

FINALLY...

ズ　ウウウウ *fwoooo*

ARMIN...

...

IF WE PROVE OURSELVES IN THIS FIRST BATTLE, THEY'LL MAKE US FRESH RECRUITS...

I MEAN, BEFORE APPLYING FOR THE SURVEY CORPS...

THIS IS A GOOD OPPORTUNITY, DON'T YOU THINK?

YEAH... NO DOUBT.

...

...AND WATCH HOW FAST WE GET PROMOTED UP THE LADDER!!

SORRY TO BURST YOUR BUBBLE...

...BUT A LOT OF PEOPLE FROM OUR CLASS ARE APPLYING FOR THE SURVEY CORPS!!

THIS IS NO TIME TO CATCH YOUR BREATH!! TOO DANGER-OUS!

H-HEY...

HIS LEG...

NO... EREN...

...DO I... WHY...

... MY COM-RADES BEING EATEN?

...HAVE TO WATCH...

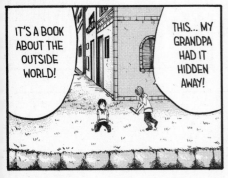

IT'S A BOOK ABOUT THE OUTSIDE WORLD!

THIS... MY GRANDPA HAD IT HIDDEN AWAY!

WHAT'S UP, ARMIN?

SO HERE YOU ARE!!

EREN!

ACCORDING TO THE BOOK, **THE MAJORITY OF THIS WORLD IS COVERED BY WATER CALLED THE "SEA"!!**

THIS IS MUCH MORE IMPORTANT THAN THAT!!

A BOOK ABOUT THE OUTSIDE WORLD?! THAT'S ILLEGAL! YOU'RE GONNA GET CAUGHT BY THE MP BRIGADE!

NO, THAT'S THE THING! THE "SEA" IS SO HUGE, IT CAN'T BE DEPLETED!

THAT'S JUST SILLY...

...

L-LIAR!! I MEAN, SALT?! THAT WOULD BE A TREASURE TROVE! MERCHANTS WOULD'VE ALREADY EXHAUSTED THE SUPPLY!!

...!! SALT?!

AND IT SAYS THE "SEA" IS ALL SALT WATER!!

...!!

THE OUTSIDE WORLD MUST BE TEN TIMES BIGGER THAN INSIDE THE WALL!

AND FIELDS OF SAND!

AND ICE GROUND!

THERE'S FIRE WATER!

AND IT'S NOT JUST A HEAP OF SALT!!

...GET TO EXPLORE THE OUTSIDE WORLD!

SOMEDAY... I HOPE WE...

EREN!

THE OUTSIDE WORLD...

HEY... ARMIN...

YOU...

THINK I'M... GONNA DIE HERE... ?

SO I'M... GOING TO THE OUTSIDE WORLD...

YOU TOLD ME ABOUT IT...

QUICKLY!!

EREN!!

CHOMP

WAAAAA!

GULP

Continued in Volume 2

ULTRA-SPECIAL BONUS!!*

DANGER! THIS INTERVIEW WITH "ATTACK ON TITAN" CREATOR HAJIME ISAYAMA CONTAINS SPOILERS FOR FUTURE VOLUMES!

Japanese readers sent in questions to ask Mr. Isayama, and his editor asked him a few. Here we present his answers. Just be careful: Some of them contain major spoilers for later volumes! We recommend you read Vol. 2, then come back and read this interview.

EDITOR: Thank you for being here today. We've received a lot of questions from the readers. Please answer to the best of your ability.
MR. ISAYAMA: I have a feeling most of my answers will be boring, but... fire away. Nothing is taboo.

Then let's begin. "Why did you decide on giants as the theme of this work?"
ISA: Well, giants are kind of gross, aren't they? That's why.

"Has anything in your life changed since the series has become so popular?"
ISA: I got a weird phone call from my bank. They were wondering about the sudden increase of funds in my savings, so they probably thought I was running some bank transfer scam. (Laughs.)

"Do you have a way to clear out the cobwebs when you're tired or when you need to decide some important story point?"
ISA: Shadowboxing with the hanging lamp cord in my house is very soothing.

"What made you decide to become a manga artist?"
ISA: I just decided one day, is all. I had a habit of doodling and daydreaming anyway, so I was fortunate that my interests were compatible with something that's profitable.

"Mr. Isayama, what is your fetish?"
ISA: I have a body hair fetish.

"How do you get over those times when making manga gets tough?"
ISA: I don't. (Laughs.) I think it's always equal parts tough and fun.

"Where do you get your ideas for stories?"
ISA: This doesn't have to do with creating stories, but when I'm half-awake, like just before I drift off to sleep, my mind gets flooded with information I've seen or heard subconsciously. I call it "Super Enlightenment Time." And this is true, I'm not kidding.

On to the next question... "Is there a manga artist whom you respect?"

ISA: There are plenty of them. Of course, there are my fellow manga artists in Betsu Maga, but also Tsutomu Nihei, Ryoji Minagawa, Kentaro Miura, Hideki Arai, Tooru Mitsumine, and I could go on and on. I'm still a fledgling.

A signed sketch by an artist Mr. Isayama respects, Mr. Nihei. It's a treasured possession that hangs on his wall.

"Who is your favorite character in Attack on Titan?"

ISA: That would be Jean. Jean comes right out and says what he's thinking, even if it's something you normally couldn't say. That's what I like about him.

"Out of all the manga you've read, what influenced you most?"

ISA: ARMS.

"How far ahead do you have Attack on Titan plotted out?"

ISA: In broad strokes, I've got it pretty well thought out to way, way down the line. And I've got outlines that say like, such-and-such a truth will be revealed in volume 5 and around volume 10, this situation is going to happen. See, if I didn't decide these things before it sees publication, I wouldn't even be able to come up with ideas. Although I don't flesh it out until I'm actually working on it...

Jean Kirstein. I like the name, too.

"What do you think of Miyajima (Masanori Miyajima)?"

ISA: He's got a permanent crease on his nose from his glasses.

"Aren't you going to have female Titans?"

ISA: I wonder if I should say this... They're rare.

"I always forget how the kanji for 'Isa' in your last name goes. Is there a good way to remember how to write it?"

ISA: You can write it however. I'll answer either way.

"Mr. Isayama, I want to see where you work!"

ISA: That's the one thing I hope you'll cut me some slack on! I really don't want to show you, since it's a mess...

"If you were on a desert island and could only have three things, what would you choose besides me and a guitar?"

ISA: Other than you and a guitar, I guess I would bring a U.S. military fleet.

"Mr. Isayama, what were you like as a child?"

ISA: I don't really want to recall my childhood...

"Do you use a model for the Titans?"

ISA: For the Titan version of Eren, I use martial artist Yuushin Okami's body as a model. My ideal is the physique of a middleweight mixed martial artist. I only use the shape of the body as a model.

"I'm guessing that drawing Titans after a long time would do things to your mind. Do you have nightmares about them?"

ISA: I don't think giants are really scary in the first place, so no, never.

We went ahead and took photos of Mr. Isayama's studio.

"What's the scariest thing in the world?"
ISA: A bunch of middle school girls looking at me and going, "Eww" while laughing.

"Please tell me your basic one-month schedule."
ISA: I take a week to storyboard and three weeks to draw.

"Mikasa is always wearing the scarf she got from Eren. Doesn't she get hot?"
ISA: She doesn't wear it when it's hot outside.

"Mr. Isayama, at what age did you start drawing?"
ISA: I have a memory of being praised for a drawing I did of a dragon when I was in kindergarten.

"Are you ever mistaken for the artist who does (soccer series) Giant Killing?"
ISA: Just recently, my own editor made that mistake.

"What manga do you recommend right now?"
ISA: All-Rounder Meguru and Iron Wind!!

"Mr. Isayama, which Attack on Titan character most resembles you?"
ISA: Hmm... Mr. Hannes and the Garrison soldiers in volume I who sit around drinking booze.

Yūshin Okami, whom Mr. Isayama uses as a model.

"Is there a story that you want to do after finishing Attack on Titan?"
ISA: There's a story I've had in my mind since high school. If I get lucky enough for it to be published someday, I hope everyone reads it!

"Do you have a favorite scene in Attack on Titan?"
ISA: The scene where the TV studio gets taken over and rock music plays. Sorry...

These Garrison soldiers drink alcohol in the middle of the afternoon. Surely Mr. Isayama doesn't do *that* at work?!

"What's your favorite food?"
ISA: I'm not really into food.**

"How do you spend your free time?"
ISA: Drooling as I surf the net.

"What would you look like if you were a Titan, Mr. Isayama?"
ISA: I'm sure I'd look something like this. (Laughs.)

Thank you very much! One last question. "From what page does the story really get going?"
ISA: Just wait for the 420th page and up! Please keep reading!

* This interview originally appeared in Bessatsu Shonen Magazine December 2010 issue.
** Apparently, if he's not careful, he'll drop to 40 kilos [88 lbs] without realizing it...

Scary in a way...

Preview of

Attack on Titan,

volume 2

We're pleased to present a preview from **Attack on Titan,** volume 2, now available from Kodansha Comics. See our Web site (www.kodanshacomics.com) for details!

CHK
CHK
CHKCHK

GLISH

DRAG
DRAG
DRAG
DRAG

WHUMP

ULP
...

KER-
CHAK

SLISH

HURRY UP AND LOAD THE GRAPE-SHOT!!

LOOK AROUND! IT'S OBVIOUS, IDIOT! AND WE DON'T HAVE ANY MORE TIME TO PAMPER HIM!

BOOM

SHUT UP! ARMIN DIDN'T SAY ANYTHING ABOUT THAT!!

BOOM

OH, LEAVE IT, CONNIE! THEY'VE BEEN WIPED OUT EXCEPT FOR THIS GUY!

HEY... CALM DOWN! ARMIN! WHERE IS EVERYONE?

...BUT RESCUING THIS LOSER ISN'T WORTH THE SACRIFICES OF EREN AND THE REST.

I'M SORRY HE ENCOUNTERED MULTIPLE TITANS...

THEY PROBABLY THOUGHT HE WAS ALREADY A CORPSE.

WHY IS ARMIN THE ONLY ONE WHO MADE IT?!

BOTH OF YOU, STOP IT!!

HOW ABOUT I MAKE IT SO YOU NEVER SAY A DAMN WORD EVER AGAIN!

HEY, YOU STUPID BITCH ...

AFTER THIS MISSION IS OVER, MARRY ME!

! THAT'S MY KRISTA!

I MEAN, SUDDENLY A BUNCH OF OUR FRIENDS ARE DEAD... OF COURSE WE'RE UPSET!

EVERYONE IS FRAZZLED!!

TRUE... SHE'S CLOWNING AROUND EVEN MORE THAN USUAL...

CAN YOU STAND UP, ARMIN?

ANYWAY, WE CAN'T JUST LEAVE HIM HERE...

ORDERS ARE TO MOVE FORWARD...

LET'S GO, CONNIE.

...

ARMIN!

I'LL MEET UP WITH THE REAR-GUARD!

I'M SORRY I CAUSED PROBLEMS!

THERE'S NO WAY I CAN HOLD OUT...

...IN THIS HELL.

THIS IS IT FOR ME...

WHOOOSH

WHOOOSH

NO... THAT'S WRONG... IT HASN'T *BECOME* HELL HERE.

I'VE JUST MISUNDERSTOOD UP UNTIL NOW.

THIS WORLD...

...HAS ALWAYS BEEN HELL.

THE STRONG EAT THE WEAK.

THE WORLD'S SO EASY TO UNDERSTAND, IT'S ALMOST OBLIGING...

HIRO MASHIMA IS BACK! JOIN THE CREATOR OF *FAIRY TAIL* AS HE TAKES TO THE STARS FOR ANOTHER THRILLING SAGA!

A high-flying space adventure! All the steadfast friendship and wild fighting you've been waiting for...IN SPACE!

At Granbell Kingdom, an abandoned amusement park, Shiki has lived his entire life among machines. But one day, Rebecca and her cat companion Happy appear at the park's front gates. Little do these newcomers know that this is the first human contact Granbell has had in a hundred years! As Shiki stumbles his way into making new friends, his former neighbors stir at an opportunity for a robo-rebellion... And when his old homeland becomes too dangerous, Shiki must join Rebecca and Happy on their spaceship and escape into the boundless cosmos.

The adorable new odd-couple cat comedy manga from the creator of the beloved *Chi's Sweet Home*, in full color!

Sue & Tai-chan

Konami Kanata

Sue is an aging housecat who's looking forward to living out her life in peace... but her plans change when the mischievous black tomcat Tai-chan enters the picture! Hey! Sue never signed up to be a catsitter! *Sue & Tai-chan* is the latest from the reigning meow-narch of cute kitty comics, Konami Kanata.

THE SWEET SCENT OF LOVE IS IN THE AIR! FOR FANS OF OFFBEAT ROMANCES LIKE *WOTAKOI*

Sweat and Soap © Kintetsu Yamada / Kodansha Ltd.

In an office romance, there's a fine line between sexy and awkward... and that line is where Asako — a woman who sweats copiously — meets Koutarou — a perfume developer who can't get enough of Asako's, er, scent. Don't miss a romcom manga like no other!

KC KODANSHA COMICS

◄ KAMOME ►
SHIRAHAMA

Witch Hat Atelier

A magical manga adventure for fans of Disney and Studio Ghibli!

Witch Hat Atelier © Kamome Shirahama/Kodansha

The magical adventure that took Japan by storm is finally here, from acclaimed DC and Marvel cover artist Kamome Shirahama!

In a world where everyone takes wonders like magic spells and dragons for granted, Coco is a girl with a simple dream: She wants to be a witch. But everybody knows magicians are born, not made, and Coco was not born with a gift for magic. Resigned to her un-magical life, Coco is about to give up on her dream to become a witch…until the day she meets Qifrey, a mysterious, traveling magician. After secretly seeing Qifrey perform magic in a way she's never seen before, Coco soon learns what everybody "knows" might not be the truth, and discovers that her magical dream may not be as far away as it may seem…

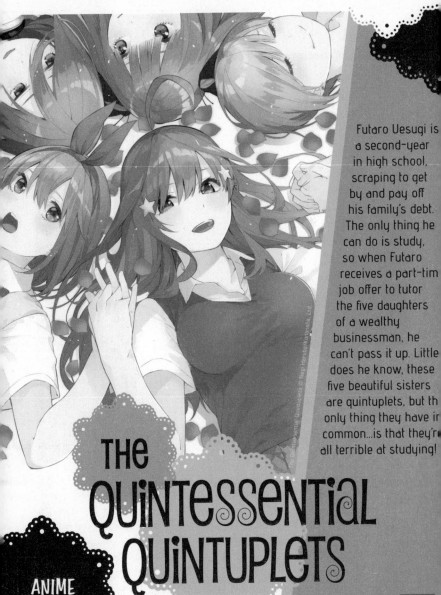

Futaro Uesugi is a second-year in high school, scraping to get by and pay off his family's debt. The only thing he can do is study, so when Futaro receives a part-tim job offer to tutor the five daughters of a wealthy businessman, he can't pass it up. Little does he know, these five beautiful sisters are quintuplets, but th only thing they have ir common...is that they'r all terrible at studying!

THE QUINTESSENTIAL QUINTUPLETS

negi haruba

ANIME OUT NOW!

Magus of the Library

Mitsu Izumi

MITSU IZUMI'S STUNNING ARTWORK BRINGS A FANTASTICAL LITERARY ADVENTURE TO LUSH, THRILLING LIFE!

Young Theo adores books, but the prejudice and hatred of his village keeps them ever out of his reach. Then one day, he chances to meet Sedona, a traveling librarian who works for the great library of Aftzaak, City of Books, and his life changes forever...

PERFECT WORLD

Rie Aruga

A TOUCHING NEW SERIES ABOUT LOVE AND COPING WITH DISABILITY

An office party reunites Tsugumi with her high school crush Itsuki. He's realized his dream of becoming an architect, but along the way, he experienced a spinal injury that put him in a wheelchair. Now Tsugumi's rekindled feelings will butt up against prejudices she never considered — and Itsuki will have to decide if he's ready to let someone into his heart...

"Depicts with great delicacy and courage the difficulties some with disabilities experience getting involved in romantic relationships... Rie Aruga refuses to romanticize, pushing her heroine to face the reality of disability. She invites her readers to the same tasks of empathy, knowledge and recognition."
—Slate.fr

"An important entry [in manga romance]... The emotional core of both plot and characters indicates thoughtfulness... [Aruga's] research is readily apparent in the text and artwork, making this feel like a real story."
—Anime News Network

KC/ KODANSHA COMICS

Knight of the Ice ©Yayoi Ogawa

Yayoi Ogawa

SKATING THRILLS AND ICY CHILLS WITH THIS NEW TINGLY ROMANCE SERIES!

A rom-com on ice, perfect for fans of *Princess Jellyfish* and *Wotakoi*. Kokoro is the talk of the figure-skating world, winning trophies and hearts. But little do they know... he's actually a huge nerd! From the beloved creator of *You're My Pet* (*Tramps Like Us*).

Chitose is a serious young woman, working for the health magazine *SASSO*. Or at least, she would be, if she wasn't constantly getting distracted by her childhood friend, international figure skating star Kokoro Kijinami! In the public eye and on the ice, Kokoro is a gallant, flawless knight, but behind his glittery costumes and breathtaking spins lies a secret: He's actually a hopelessly romantic otaku, who can only land his quad jumps when Chitose is on hand to recite a spell from his favorite magical girl anime!

Masahiro Setagawa doesn't believe in heroes, but wishes he could: He's found himself in a gang of small-time street bullies, and with no prospects for a real future. But when high school teacher (and scourge of the streets) Kousuke Ohshiba comes to his rescue, he finds he may need to start believing after all... in heroes, and in his budding feelings, too.

Hitorijime My Hero

Memeco Arii

KC KODANSHA COMICS

A dark and sexy body-horror action manga perfect for fans of *Prison School* and *High School of the Dead*!

Shuichi Kagaya is a smart kid, and most smart kids his age would be thinking about college. Shuichi is also a monster, and he's smart enough to know that monsters don't go to college. But after he uses his monstrous form to save his classmate Claire Aoki, it doesn't matter what his plans for the future were, because he's not the one making the decisions anymore. Now that the seductive, sadistic Claire knows Shuichi's secret, she's got her own ideas about what a monster is good for—because he's not the first monster she's met...

KC
KODANSHA
COMICS

GLEIPNIR

"You and me together...we would be unstoppable."

Something's Wrong With Us

NATSUMI ANDO

The dark, psychological, sexy shojo series readers have been waiting for!

A spine-chilling and steamy romance between a Japanese sweets maker and the man who framed her mother for murder!

Following in her mother's footsteps, Nao became a traditional Japanese sweets maker, and with unparalleled artistry and a bright attitude, she gets an offer to work at a world-class confectionary company. But when she meets the young, handsome owner, she recognizes his cold stare...

KC KODANSHA COMICS

Young characters and steampunk setting, like *Howl's Moving Castle* and *Battle Angel Alita*

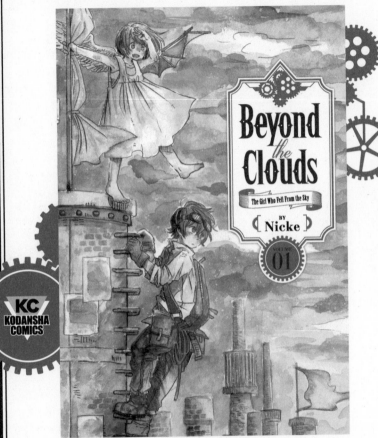

Beyond the Clouds © 2018 Nicke / Ki-oon

A boy with a talent for machines and a mysterious girl whose wings he's fixed will take you beyond the clouds! In the tradition of the high-flying, resonant adventure stories of Studio Ghibli comes a gorgeous tale about the longing of young hearts for adventure and friendship!

A Kodansha Comics Trade Paperback Original

Attack on Titan volume 1 copyright © 2010 Hajime Isayama
English translation copyright © 2012 Hajime Isayama

All rights reserved.

Published in the United States by Kodansha Comics, an imprint of Kodansha USA Publishing, LLC, New York.

Publication rights for this English edition arranged through Kodansha Ltd, Tokyo.

First published in Japan in 2010 by Kodansha Ltd., Tokyo.

ISBN 978-1-64651-448-9

Original cover design by Takashi Shimoyama (Red Rooster)

Printed in Italy by Grafica Veneta S.p.A.

www.kodanshacomics.com

Translator: Sheldon Drzka
Lettering: Steve Wands

You are going the *wrong way!*

Manga is a *completely* different type of reading experience.

To start at the *BEGINNING,* go to the *END!*

That's right! Authentic manga is read the traditional Japanese way—from right to left, exactly the opposite of how American books are read. It's easy to follow: just go to the other end of the book, and read each page—and each panel—from the right side to the left side, starting at the top right. Now you're experiencing manga as it was meant to be.